MW01114467

# PREPARE
# FOR
# CONTACT

## A Guide For Interacting
## With Galactic Beings

Tamara Scott Crowley

Galactic Ambassador Press

# PREFACE

We are the children of the Cosmos. It is wonderful that a writer like Tamara Scott Crowley can integrate her wisdom and sensitivity in this intergalactic handbook. Contact is not a simple action and as we know from the Eastern spiritual traditions in Buddhism and Vedic cultures, the process engages the entire human being.
 We must clear the mind and the body first. They are not separate. This book is a roadmap to a faster and more effective communication with Cosmic Cultures.

This book gives us a practical and simple application of how to do that. Communication with the Cosmos begins first with communication with ourselves, our inner soul. Tamara has been a student of the process for many years and is able to address so many of these issues. She is a traveler in many realms. She sees a simple path to achieve this oneness with the universe. Dr. Edgar Michell (Apollo 14 astronaut ) was able to achieve this "epiphany,' this vision of oneness, while traveling in Space to the moon.

Nonhuman intelligence has been trying to contact humanity for many years. We are them. They are us and it is time we begin to learn, to go to school, to graduate into a realm of consciousness. It is a matter of survival for our species. It is a matter of wonderment. Welcome to her world as you go on this journey. Bon Voyage.

**Paola Leopizzi Harris**
International photojournalist and investigative reporter in the area of extraterrestrial related phenomenon research, renowned author, and Producer of the Starworks USA conference in Laughlin, NV.
www.startworksusa.com

This book is dedicated to two amazing men in my life. My husband, Bill Crowley, and my best friend, Don Rich.

Without your love, support, guidance, generosity and the sharing of your gifts, Galactic Ambassadors and this book would never have happened. I am forever grateful to both of you for 'always having my back!'

Tamara Scott Crowley

# Table of Contents

# BRING YOUR CURIOSITY

# CHAPTER ONE

# Prepare For Contact

We are not alone, and we never have been.

Since the beginning of time, the indigenous native populations around the world all share their "creation stories" that talk about their origins in the heavens, and visits and guidance from the "star people." They understand that "humans" were seeded on planet Earth for many different purposes and reasons – and by many different species from non-Earth origins.

At this very moment, there are people living amongst us who look human, but their DNA is not exclusively human, or human at all. How could this even be possible?

The future proves the past. We have been on an evolutionary time loop that just keeps going on and on and on. As the saying goes, "the more things change, the more they stay the same." We have had key opportunities throughout the ages where we, as a collective, could come together to raise our consciousness and break this cycle. We could overcome our fear, anger, greed and self-centered tendencies to raise our vibration enough to break the cycle.

Instead, we fall back into the same old patterns, and we willfully relinquish our sovereignty to a small handful of narcissistic, egoic people who rule us through all of the lower-vibration control mechanisms in exchange for what?

There will come a time when we meet other races in our daily life, and I don't mean humans from different ancestral origins.

In the not so distant future, it will be common to interact with species entirely outside of the human spectrum. Aquatic-beings, Reptilians, Insectoids, Tall Whites, Nordics, and a complete range of other beings that are from other planets that support life.

As a human species, we already struggle to unconditionally respect others of our own race that represent different skin colors, cultures, sex, sexual orientation, religious preferences, educational levels, and socio-economic status. Can you imagine how planet Earth would react to meeting a wide range of new intelligent species that are non-human? I do, which is why I have written this book.

The goal is to provide you with the basic skills to approach a non-human being, and to build a relationship with that individual from a place of unconditional respect.

There are also important tools and techniques that can prepare you for an encounter with an inner-earth or galactic citizen. While some of our alien friends are similar to us, they also have a lot of differences that can be quite shocking or downright scary. This guide can help to reduce the anxieties and provide you with confidence when meeting a non-human for the first time.

Just remember, they may be just as afraid of you, as you may be of them!

Congratulations on taking the first step in becoming a good Earth Ambassador, and a galactic citizen.

# CHAPTER TWO

# Similarities And Differences Between Humans & Non-Humans

When people on Earth are considering travelling to another country, it is always beneficial to study the indigenous culture and customs. This gives you context for appreciating the travel experience, while honoring the traditions of the area that you are exploring. The same concept applies when you are preparing to make contact with non-human beings.

We all have similarities and differences, and it is important to honor all aspects that make up a human or non-human.

If you are new to considering what other beings that are not from Earth may be like, here is a quick rundown of the basics:

| EARTH HUMANS | NON-HUMANS |
|---|---|
| Use money | Don't use money |
| Use petroleum and other fossil fuels | Use high-tech propulsion systems |
| Have basic technology for machines, equipment, medical needs and vehicles. Are mechanical in nature and are not conscious. | Have extremely advanced technology for medical needs, transportation, equipment, etc. Their technology is conscious and interacts with the user. Requires a high degree of consciousness to operate. |

| EARTH HUMANS | NON-HUMANS |
|---|---|
| Demonstrate lower levels of consciousness | Demonstrate higher levels of consciousness |
| Have a 3D physical body with a head, two arms and two legs. | May or may not have a physical body; or may utilize a "temporary" body to materialize. These may be in various forms and configurations. |
| Use various modes of transportation that includes cars, trains, planes, etc. to navigate to locations on Earth. | Use high-tech spacecraft to travel interdimensionally or may utilize wormholes or portals for time travel. May also travel without any type of craft, but by using their consciousness through bi-location or tri-location. |
| Believe in various religions or are agnostic | Believe in "oneness" and/or a divine source. |
| Are concerned about themselves or their family. | Are concerned about everyone as a whole. |
| Use many verbal languages in various dialects to communicate, which will require translation if you don't speak the language. | May have a "native" language but can communicate telepathically, which will automatically be understood by any other being without translation. |

| EARTH HUMANS | NON-HUMANS |
|---|---|
| Eat all types of food (fruit, veggies, meat, starches, etc.) to maintain the physical body. | Some beings live on energy or "prana" while others may eat fruit/vegetarian-based meals, and a few eat meat. |
| Procreate and may have children / families. | Some procreate and have families. |
| Have jobs to earn money and support themselves and their families. | Apply their interests to serve their community, which serves everyone. |
| Educate their children in formal institutions using standardized methods and curriculum; some home schooling. | Educate their children through various methods of osmosis, home schooling, sharing of consciousness. |
| Have entertainment, such as music, movies, sports, etc. | Have various forms of entertainment, including music and some games. |

As we prepare for contact with other species, it is always appropriate to look for our similarities. Non-humans have a strong sense of connectedness to their family, their species, and all of consciousness. They have offspring and educate their children, while they serve their communities with their individual gifts, skills and training. They enjoy leisure time, music and some have a great sense of humor.

Let's get ready to meet our galactic neighbors!

# RAISE YOUR CONSCIOUSNESS

CHAPTER THREE

# Consciousness: The Path To "Contact"

Civilizations outside of Earth are more advanced technologically and spiritually. In order to interact with our galactic neighbors, they have to lower their consciousness and we have to raise our consciousness to try to "meet somewhere in the middle."

## So, what is consciousness?

The definition of consciousness, according to the dictionary, is:

> 1.the state of being **conscious**; awareness of one's own existence,
> sensations, thoughts, surroundings, etc.

In addition, to "raise one's consciousness" is:

> 1. to increase one's awareness and understanding of one's own needs, behavior, attitudes, etc., especially
> as a member of a particular social or political group.

If you look at the definitions by academics, philosophers and scientists, you will find differing opinions, but it generally all boils down to:

**An infinite field of energy that includes all forms and the history and potential of all existence.**

## Why is it important?

As a species, we have grown and evolved physically, socially and mentally at various rates over the centuries. At this point in our collective development, many realize that the human species is not alone in the universe, and that there are "others out there" who are far more evolved than we are.

From a spiritual or religious perspective, humans have revered and worshiped beings or deities with 'higher states of consciousness" since the beginning of time. There have been ongoing reports of visitations, prophecies, messages and miracles from angels, ascended masters, and gurus, just to name a few. The basic premise of all religions is to elevate ones self to become more "Godlike" or continual enlightenment.

As the Earth moves closer to "full disclosure" of our collective government's interactions and visitations with species from outside of our galaxy (and from inner Earth,) individuals are asking what they need to do to prepare themselves and others for contact.

Basically, we have a present level of consciousness, can raise our consciousness and are an integral part of infinite consciousness. How we identify with ourselves and life depends on our own consciousness level.

One important step is to evaluate where you currently are on the consciousness continuum. This can be done by examining your current behaviors, attitudes or beliefs, determining which are limiting to your growth, and then replace them with new, higher behaviors. Easier said than done!

## How do you do it?

If there were a simple, easy answer to increase consciousness that fit everyone, then we all would have done it by now!

There is no one path, no "magic pill," and it certainly does not happen over night. Every individual is unique and has different challenges and struggles to overcome in this current existence. What may be a challenge for one person is not for another. So, a "one size fits all approach" does not work. Before we get into the specifics, though, there is one factor that must be present:

# You Have To Want To
# Raise Your Consciousness

No one can do it for you, and the work is 100% an "inside job." That said, you can ask others to help guide you through various aspects of your self enhancement project. They may provide tools, techniques, resources, nutritional guidance, etc., but at the end of the day, the only person that can fix you, is YOU.

Below are some items that I believe are fundamental to raising consciousness:

Emotional Related:
> Are you loving and forgiving to yourself and others?
> Have you identified and healed your "core wounds?"
> Do you meditate/pray at least twice daily?
> Are you free from addictions (e.g., drugs, alcohol, shopping, food, television, etc.)?

Health Related:
> Have you shifted your diet to "high vibration" (e.g., live, whole foods) and organic?
> Do you drink enough water to total half of your body weight in ounces every day?
> Do you have a regular sleep cycle with at least 7 hours of sleep?
> Do you consistently breathe from the diaphragm, not your chest?
> Do you exercise regularly?

Spiritual Related:
> Are you continually seeking to raise your consciousness? Basically, are you growing or are you dying?
> Are you willing to question all of your current beliefs, while using discernment in validating potential new paradigms?
> And, finally, there are ultimately only two emotions: Love and fear. LOVE is the most powerful energy in the multi-verse.

The next chapters will take you through some of the key areas to focus upon to raise consciousness and support contact with our galactic neighbors.

# CHAPTER FOUR

# What You Eat And Drink Impacts Your Vibration

**""Let food be thy medicine and medicine be thy food."**

**Hippocrates**

While clearing and cleaning out your "human vessel," it is imperative to look at the fuel that you are using to power yourself.

When we look at addiction, food and non-alcoholic beverages are the easiest, cheapest and completely legal drugs to consume. After all, who is going to pull you over and arrest you for eating a jelly donut?

I am a self-confessed sugar addict. When I was a kid, I would wait until my mom was on the phone and then sneak into the kitchen to eat sugar out of the sugar bowl with a spoon. Butter and sugar on white Wonder Bread was the ultimate snack and Halloween and Easter were all about the candy!

When it comes to raising your consciousness, it is all about what you put into your body – and what you DON'T put into your body.

Let's start with the basics:
- Drink your water:
    - One ounce of purified, filtered water for half of your body weight in ounces. So, if you weigh 150 pounds, you need to drink 75 ounces of water a day.
- Chew your food well:
    - Your stomach does not have teeth!
- Breathe:
    - Inhale into the diaphragm, not the chest.

Now, as for the fuel...lets also start with the basics:
- Organic foods
- Non-GMO
- As close to nature as possible. These are simple, live foods that are not processed.

Do you see any junk food or fast food on the list? Nope.

Eliminate the following:
- White or brown refined sugar
- All sugar substitutes (e.g., aspartame, etc.)
- Fast food
- Processed junk food (e.g., cookies, cakes, candies, chips, soda, etc.)

Limit the following:
- Dairy
- Wheat
- Gluten
- Alcohol
- Caffeine
- Meat

Food vibrates at various frequencies, with organic fruits and vegetables being the highest on the scale. It is also important to eat foods that are alkaline, versus acidic.

If you are eating a "Standard American Diet" of breads, desserts, sodas, fast food, etc., then you have an opportunity to refine your diet one food category at a time. Don't go all crazy and hard-core at once. It won't stick. This is a process where you should eliminate ONE item at a time. Say, for instance, that you like to drink soda and you are willing to give it up. Decide that you are going to give up soda and pick alternate drinks to select when you go to a restaurant. It could be water, or unsweetened iced tea. Do it for one week and see how you are doing. Was it easy? Do you feel deprived? Note how your body feels, and whether you are missing the sugar/ artificial sweeteners / caffeine / carbonation.

If you don't have any cravings or miss it, then select another item to remove from your diet that you want to change (e.g., fast food) and then repeat the process. Find healthier alternatives to replace the item that you loved.

I have to confess that I gave up sugar many, many times. I would go four or five months without it and then I would find myself in the middle of an entire chocolate cake with a fork. I would make myself sick! It would make me feel so incredibly ill, as I am hypoglycemic, and this would completely screw up my blood sugar. Then, the sugar roller coaster would begin and I'd get on the high and start coming down, and then need more sugar to go up again. UGH! It truly was a demon in my life.

I was able to find alternatives to sugar that could replace the cravings – and over time, the longer that I was not eating sugar, the better I felt.  I truly believe that sugar is more addicting than cocaine.  A prominent California Endocrinologist, Dr. Robert Lustig's research supports that belief, and the article is footnoted below for reference. [1]

As you refine your diet, PLEASE read all labels for food that you purchase at the grocery store.  Sugar is hidden in everything and added to foods so that you crave more of it.  Restaurants also use a lot of sugar to enhance their food and it is put into sauces, dressings and basic recipes.  If you are eating out, ask for organic meats that are grilled and vegetables with butter, only (no sauce).   Ditto for the salad....order it without dressing and get fresh lemons and olive oil on the side.  Always ask, "What is in this?" before ordering.

As you continue to eat a "clean diet," your body will evolve and transform.  Your tastes for different foods will change and you will crave healthy, organic food.  Over time, you will eat less food as your body receives the nutrients that it needs from whole foods.

Explore different types of food and the way it is prepared.  No two people are alike, so a raw, vegan diet may work for one person, but another may need to eat organic meat and eggs each week to feel optimum.  I know that is the case for me.  I tried to go 100% vegetarian, and also raw/vegan, but my body needed the protein from meat and eggs.  One of the best books that I read was "Beyond Broccoli: Creating a

---

[1] http://www.nydailynews.com/life-style/health/researcher-sugar-addictive-cocaine-obesity-diabetes-cancer-heart-disease-article-1.1054419/

biologically balanced diet when a vegetarian diet doesn't work," by Susan Schenck.

Here is a common theme that will keep repeating throughout this book: "Go within to see what resonates with you!" Check in to see how foods affect your mood, emotions, weight, digestion, etc." No two people are exactly the same, so you are going to have to "play detective" to see what works for you. I have tried the Candida Yeast Diet, Blood Type diet, Mediterranean diet, Keto diet, raw/vegan diet, vegetarian diet, Weight Watchers diet, and the Standard American diet (by default from birth.) Some were a total disaster, while others worked for a while and then were not as effective.

Overall, the diet that works the best for me is the Candida Yeast Diet. It is sensible, easy to follow, and the food is delicious. I have been able to eat out in restaurants and modify "Standard American Diet" recipe favorites to fit the guidelines.

At the end of the day, it all comes down to eating what fuel will support your body, while not overdoing the calories. It's about feeling great, lowering the inflammation in the body, and taking care of yourself – which is the vehicle for your spirit/soul while you are on earth.

As an adult, I have weighed 206 pounds at my heaviest and 122 at my lightest, and have weighed everywhere in between. I know the struggle of weight loss and the battle of weight gain. I have also had lovely periods in my life of weight maintenance, and those were attributable to a consistent, healthy diet, lots of water, good sleeping habits, stable hormones, low stress levels and regular exercise. It can be a challenge to manage all of those factors, but by balancing all of them, you will be able to increase your physical and mental health.

Make sure to check out the reference section for recommended sources on diet and some fantastic cookbooks.

CHAPTER FIVE

# Exercise Is Imperative
# For Overall Health

True confession: I would rather sit in my zero-gravity
recliner with an amazing book, drinking a cup of tea
with my cat sleeping on my lap than exercise.

However, a human's physical body is designed to be
maintained through exercise, in addition to a healthy,
live-food diet. Keeping the body moving ensures that
your entire energy field is healthy, and that your
physical body is pain and inflammation free. It is also
imperative to keep the lymphatic system flowing
smoothly to help with the elimination of toxins.

The health of your physical body can greatly enhance
your abilities to raise your consciousness and facilitate
contact with our space neighbors. It's part of an entire
ecosystem that needs to be in balance in order to raise
your overall energetic vibration.

Simple exercise will do! Walking five or more times
per week for 30 minutes a day is great. Yoga, Tai-chi,
Chi-gong, stretching, and some light weights are
wonderful. Swimming is fantastic, and can also be
meditative. Ride a bike around the neighborhood,
or on a local bike path or park trail.

Try to spend at least 30 minutes a day moving. More
is better. Try out new forms of exercise that you are
interested in exploring. My next adventure is to try
out Pilates that uses the Reformer machines to help
with toning and lengthening the muscles while
stretching and remaining limber. Find activities that

you love, and you will continue to remain active throughout your life.

CHAPTER SIX

# The Magic Of Sleep

Sleep is a requirement for humans, and some need more than others.

Personally, I like to get at least eight hours of sleep each night to feel my best. It is important to try to establish a set bedtime each night and have a regular schedule, if possible. This allows the body to regulate and repair itself, while you are off on a marvelous dream adventure.

There are also other important things that happen when you sleep that the mainstream media doesn't talk about. This includes the chance for your consciousness to travel outside of your body and either "return" to its energy form in the spirit world, OR the opportunity to learn and experience adventures in various places and dimensions. Yes, that's right! Your consciousness is on a field trip while your physical body is undergoing nightly rejuvenation, and is connected with a silver filament cord that connects through the top of your head.

Have you ever had one of those dreams where a noise wakes you up and you slam back into your body, and the bed bounces? (This is just like when you step on the lever on your vacuum cleaner and the retractable cord flies back into the machine and the plug smacks the opening!) Your consciousness is trying to quickly re-enter your physical body, and it has a rough re-entry due to the speed in which it needs to re-integrate. It's not harmful, just a little disorienting if you don't understand what is happening.

## SETTING THE INTENTION PRIOR TO SLEEP

Dream time is a chance to connect with non-humans in a relaxed state. You may set the intention to meet with or talk to a benevolent galactic being, travel to a space ship, or another planet.

Once in bed, simply say out loud, "I wish to connect with benevolent galactic beings tonight and remember my interaction with them when I awake," or something along those lines with your personal wishes. Then, relax and focus on your breathing while you drift off to sleep.

When you wake up in the morning, immediately journal any dreams that you may have had during the night. Keep a dream journal on your nightstand and log your thoughts, impressions and experiences before you even get out of bed, as your recollection will fade as the morning unfolds.

Sleep is a magical time that is restorative to your body, an opportunity to receive messages from your sub-conscious mind, and have mysterious encounters and adventures. Take advantage of this opportunity each day to support your overall health while exploring the unknown.

# CHAPTER SEVEN

# Meditation Will Change Your Life

In today's busy world, we are all stressed out due to constantly changing demands on our time and we don't focus our minds because we are continually distracted by technology. Televisions, computers and cell phones pull us away from engaging in an interpersonal conversation, or just being fully present in the moment.

Meditation is a foundational component to raise your consciousness, reduce stress and become more fully present in every moment of your life. In addition, numerous research studies[2] have proven that it can improve your cardiovascular health, be used to treat addictions, insomnia and PTSD, and many other afflictions.

It is also a serves a critical function when communicating telepathically with a non-human or non-corporeal being for two reasons:

1.) When you are talking telepathically to someone, you must maintain your sole focus on the conversation at hand and not start thinking about other things.

2.) You need to be able to remain calm and in a higher vibrational state to enable conversations with beings that are in different dimensions or vibrate at higher states.

---

[2] TM.org

As a psychic medium, I have telepathic communications with a client's spirit guides or their deceased relatives. Although I have been doing this work for years, there are times when I get distracted. Below is a scenario where I am receiving a validating message for a future session with my client, and my mind begins to wander:

Spirit Guide: "Penelope's favorite meal is the Greek Salad from Urth Caffe."

Tamara: Noting the message, my mind jumps to my personal grocery list and that I need to buy salad. I then catch myself, as I am focusing on MY life. I sheepishly have to bring my attention back to the Spirit Guide who is patiently waiting for me.

Spirit Guide: "Hi. Are you ready to continue?"

This is super embarrassing, as the "other side" is working hard to lower their vibration enough to communicate with me and here I am, getting distracted and not focusing on the conversation.

I have found that meditating for 20 minutes, twice a day (in the morning and evening) can help with focus, clearing the mind and thoughts, and lowering stress levels. This, in turn, helps to raise your consciousness and enable multi-dimensional communication.

I also enjoy longer global meditation sessions every Sunday where I can connect on a conscious level with many others at the same time and the focus is on world peace (see Resource section regarding meditation or visit www.sandrawalter.com.)

For me, meditation is the opportunity to go within and swim in the sea of my soul, to feel the infinite possibilities of the entire universe and connect into pure consciousness. It is the feeling of nothingness, expansiveness and the experience of unconditional love.

It is also the chance to ignore the thoughts of work that interrupt my bliss, tune out the neighbor's car alarm, and smile when the cat jumps in my lap to join in on the meditation.

Meditation will change your life.

CHAPTER EIGHT

# Detoxification & Alternative Healing Support Vitality

If you have been eating the Standard American Diet for years, have been smoking, drinking tap water, eating lots of sugar, or have been exposed to a lot of chemicals and genetically modified food, then your body may be in desperate need of detoxification.

Normally, the body is amazing at being able to clear itself of debris that inhibits perfect health.  However, if your system is overloaded with too many different toxins, then the liver, kidneys and colon can't keep up with moving these items out of your system in an efficient manner – and then inflammation and illness sets in.

There is a lot of "buzz" in the media touting the benefits of detoxification, which can include green juice fasting.  Depending upon the current state of your physical health, you may need to enlist the help of a naturopath to determine whether there are nutritional deficiencies, an overload of heavy metals, or Candida yeast overgrowth.  The doctor can determine whether you need a supplement, or a deeper detoxification in a specific area to enable your body to heal and repair itself.

When I was born, I had thrush in the eyes and mouth. Thrush is an overgrowth of Candida yeast from coming through the birth canal.  This set me up for a lifetime of craving sugar, which feeds the yeast.  Anytime I had an illness or sinus infection, I was given antibiotics by my Western medical doctor, which continued to feed the yeast and create imbalance in my body. It was a vicious cycle.

I was able to finally break the cycle by working with my naturopath to undergo a strict diet, and take a regime of supplements for two weeks that helped me to reduce the yeast overgrowth to a proper level. I quit using all synthetic fragrances, which included perfume and scented laundry soap, dryer sheets, and cleaning supplies. I also started using a NetiPot to rinse my sinus cavities to remove pollution and since then, I have never had another sinus infection.

If you don't want to consult a Naturopath or are unable to find one in your local area, there are simple things that you can do to assist your body to detoxify:

- Sit in a sauna for 10-15 minutes a couple of days each week to sweat out toxins in your system;
- Use a tongue scraper to remove excess bacteria off of your tongue;
- Floss daily and brush at least twice a day to lower bacteria levels in your mouth;
- Use a skin brush to "dry brush" your body before showering to remove dead skin cells so that your pores are open;
- Use a NetiPot and the accompanying saline packets to rinse out your sinus cavities;
- Exercise at least 30 minutes (or more) a day to get your lymphatic system moving;
- Get a massage to help clear the lymph glands;
- Get a colonic from a certified colon hydrotherapist;
- Perform water and/or coffee enemas at home on a regular basis to hydrate and assist with the removal of waste from your colon; and,

- Eliminate <u>synthetic</u> fragrances (e.g., perfume or aftershave, laundry soap, dryer sheets, room fresheners, cleaning supplies, etc.) from your personal and home use. Use only natural essential oils for personal care and fragrance, as well as the cleaning of your home.

Getting waste and toxins out of your body is just as important as what you put into or onto your body.

## COMPLIMENTARY HEALING MODALITIES

Over the years, I have tried many complimentary healing modalities, such as acupuncture, Directional Non-Force Technique (DNFT) chiropractic, colon hydrotherapy, energy medicine, massage, Reike and sound therapy. I have also worked with a Transpersonal Psychologist (which is therapy that integrates the spiritual and transcendent aspects into traditional psychotherapy) to tackle some challenging life situations. I have also done past-life regression, and hypnotherapy.

The various modalities work on the physical, emotional, mental and spiritual levels to bring the overall body into balance.

As you move through life and make a concerted effort to raise your consciousness, opportunities to use these healing therapies may present themselves to you. For example, if you keep getting repeat messages from various sources that reference acupuncture, this could be your higher self (or guides) encouraging you to investigate using this ancient healing method to assist you.

For me, colon hydrotherapy was life-changing, as I had an amazing International Association for Colon Hydrotherapy (I-Act) certified master teacher who walked me through the process. I went weekly for many years, and it completely changed my life. I lost weight, changed my diet, eliminated waste and toxins, and improved my overall health. Then, as I was continually improving my health, the rest of my life kept changing.

I evaluated my current job and career path, relationship, personal happiness, financial health, spiritual growth, etc. I made some MAJOR life changes that allowed me to better align with my soul's purpose and mission, which brought great joy to my life and an ongoing feeling of wellbeing.

Was it easy? Absolutely not! It was a lot of hard work, trial and error, and sacrifice. However, I always felt guided and supported by an invisible team of guides who kept assisting me and cheering me on.

If you make a commitment to be the absolute best version of yourself that you can be, then the Universe will rise up to meet you and provide you with the tools and resources to complete the hero's journey. You just have to pay attention, be brave, and keep going!

CHAPTER NINE

# Transparency & Truth: Retrain Your Brain

Why would telling the truth be so important?  Because telepathy and communication with non-humans is completely transparent.  If you are thinking something but are not saying it out loud, they know it.

Have you ever been in a grocery store and saw another person who weighed more than you, was dressed in weird clothes and accessories, or acted differently than you?  Did you immediately judge them based on their appearance, their behavior, or their socio-economic status?  Well, you can get away with that on Earth, but not anywhere else in the galaxy!

Every thought you produce is transmitted to anyone who is telepathic, so this can become rather embarrassing if you are staring at a being from another planet and are thinking, "Look at the color of her skin!  It's blue!  Holy crap!  What is going on with her eyes?  They are HUGE and creepy!"  She is hearing every thought you are thinking, and is (hopefully) giving you grace because you are not adept at controlling your mind and thoughts.

Transparency and truth tie in closely with meditation, with a subtle difference.  Meditation is about focusing the mind and creating stillness.  Transparency and truth is about monitoring your thoughts and actively working on being honest, while not immediately judging every thing you see, based on your personal stereotypes and preferences.

Focus, instead, on the energy that the being or person emits, rather than the physical representation of their body.

On a daily basis, challenge yourself to walk into a store or a meeting at work and practice NOT judging everyone you see. Instead, register in your mind whom you see (without judging their physical appearance) and then move your focus into your heart. From your heart, imagine a chord going from your heart to their heart and FEEL what they are feeling. Are they happy? Upset about something going on? Can you share a smile and a kind word with them?

With continued practice, you will begin to retrain your brain to stop labeling, judging and categorizing people (and our galactic neighbors), and instead, connecting on a heart and energy level that is utilized by those at higher levels of consciousness.

# CHAPTER TEN

# Home Environment: Clear the Clutter To Create Calm!

If you pay attention to the signs that your guides and the universe send you, then you will discover areas of your life that need to be addressed that were never on your radar. This happened to me. I was completely unaware that my home environment was impacting my consciousness.

I was drawn to Marie Kondo's show, "Tidying Up" on Netflix in early 2019. This Japanese dynamo of spiritual energy charmed me with her expertise in the art of "tidying," and her methodical process thrilled and horrified me at the same time. Really? Sort through ALL of my crap?? Holy cow!

Armed with an entire box of outdoor trash bags, I approached this project with an iron will and a naive perspective of what this process was going to do to my life.

The recommended method is to sort your belongings in the following order: Clothing, Books, Paper, Komono (miscellaneous in Japanese), and Sentimental Items. For each category, you must pick up each item and ask, "Does this spark joy or me?" If it does, you store it properly in a designated space. If it does not "spark joy," then you thank the item for its service, and donate or discard it.

As I was going through this process, I had a lot of thoughts swirling in my brain….like, "Why do I have all of this stuff that I don't use and need?" "How come I haven't cleaned this out before?" I donated seven outdoor trash bags full of just clothing and shoes to Goodwill!

Going through everything also helped me to clear out the "old" to prepare for the "new." I purchased new sheets and washcloths, and donated the ones that were worn and didn't "spark joy" any longer.

As I continued through this three-month process, I was shocked that I was so unconscious about what was in my physical space.

For example, I had a gift that was given to me by someone who didn't like me. I had the item in my home and used it daily. What I didn't realize was that every time I went to use the gift, it reminded me of the dislike from this person – and I was triggered on a level that wasn't even registering in my conscious mind. Over and over, I was reminded at a deep, subliminal level that I was "not lovable." Wow, all that power in one item sitting in my house. A huge epiphany hit me! I grabbed up the item, thanked it for its service and stuck it in the bag going to Goodwill.

You have to be conscious of EVERYTHING in your space, as it either feeds you or it will eat at you. The tidying process is about moving forward in your life on a spiritual level AND a physical level.

Another fascinating outcome is how easy it is to keep my house neat and clean now that everything has an assigned space. I used to have little piles of paper, clothes, and miscellaneous stuff all over the house until I went on a major cleaning binge. I would get frustrated at how cluttered everything was and then I would spend hours bringing order out of chaos. Now, everything gets put away in its proper place after it is used, and my house is always tidy. This has really provided the most amazing peace of mind and JOY when I walk into my house.

Our environments vibrate with our energy and reflect our current state on many different levels. By tidying your home, you ensure that every item surrounding you "sparks joy," creates calm and raises your consciousness.

# MAKE CONTACT

# CHAPTER ELEVEN

# Your Intention To Connect And Preparedness

Setting the intention to connect with our space neighbors is an important part of facilitating contact. By saying a daily affirmation to be open to a visit from a benevolent, non-human, you open your awareness and expand your energy field to the possibility.

An example of an intention is, "I am now connecting with benevolent Galactic beings who wish to communicate with me and my higher self in mutual service, for the highest good of all. So be it, and so it is."

You may also want to use the free, guided meditation available on the Galactic Ambassadors web site to open yourself to interaction with benevolent ET beings (www.galacticambassadors.com). This 10-minute meditation is very relaxing, in addition to setting the intention to connect. If you don't have internet connectivity or have not downloaded the MP3 file, then the written script is available in Chapter Sixteen for your reference.

Once you have set the intention to connect, then it is time to prepare for contact!

I seriously don't know if anyone is ever ready to meet an alien for the first time. You MAY think that you are ready, but when the moment comes, you may be afraid, excited, shocked by their appearance, or wondering how the heck they arrived in your physical space. Or, all of the above!

The best way to get ready for your first encounter is to treat this exactly how you would prepare for a disaster:
1. Make a plan;
2. Practice the plan; and,
3. Revise the plan after your first contact.

I have listened to many instances where people have had their first encounter with a non-human, and they feel that they didn't react how they wanted to. They were scared, surprised, overwhelmed, or just didn't know what to do. Some felt ashamed or embarrassed that they "messed up" during their meeting, and were worried that they may never get a chance again to make up for how they responded during their initial contact.

Please know that this is normal, and you will most certainly have a chance to interact again in the near future. Everyone that I have talked to had a successful second chance to interact again with the being. Think of it as a "galactic do-over!"

I also want to note that your initial contact with an alien may be in a dream (as discussed in Chapter Six), in Meditation, which would be inter-dimensional, or could occur physically on earth.

In the next chapter, we will cover some basic tools for interaction that will provide you with a solid foundation prior to your first contact experience.

# CHAPTER TWELVE

# **Tools For Interaction**

As we discussed in earlier chapters, telepathy is the primary means of communication between humans and non-humans. You can expect that this will most likely be the way that you communicate when you make contact.

This is similar to when you sleep at night and you talk to others in your dream, but you don't verbally say things out loud. You have already experienced and practiced telepathy without even realizing it! Just know that you are already an "old pro" and everything will come to you in the moment.

Many people revere aliens, as they feel that they are better than humans, are smarter, more enlightened, and have better technology. Some of those may be true, but the aliens also respect humans for their positive qualities. ET's are fascinated with our artwork, music, creativity, and especially our emotions! They usually don't exhibit a wide range of feelings and emotions, so we can be pretty entertaining to our space neighbors when we laugh, cry, or get really angry.

The point here is to retain your sovereignty. Do not give away your personal power or become enamored of another species because they have gifts or talents that are considered super-powers compared to humans. It is important to recognize that humans have gifts that are considered super-powers to other species, and we are unique to them because of it.

Your focus should be to see yourself as an equal to your new galactic friend, and see what you can learn from them, and share whatever you can with them. Think of it as an inter-stellar cultural exchange. If you can be both a teacher and a student – you open yourself for a positive and equal exchange of knowledge and information.

During your exchange, use your empathy to connect with the being. Open your heart to their energy, their intention, and feel what they are trying to share. Connect through your heart center and try to take your brain offline as much as possible. This will enrich your experience, and provide your guest with an epic encounter that they will never forget. Remember, emotions are heightened in humans, so connecting on a deep level with a human will be something extraordinary for your new friend.

Use all of your senses to take in the experience. What do they smell like? How do they look? Do you feel their happiness? Excitement? Do you taste anything in your mouth or does your body tingle? Can you touch their skin or their clothes without being rude? Use all of your faculties to have a full immersion encounter. They will also appreciate your calm curiosity and childlike wonder.

Observation is an important tool to use. Don't stare, as for some races this would be considered rude or may be a sign of aggression. However, when you can, pay attention to details. Ask appropriate questions that will not be offensive. Watch what they do and what their mannerisms are. From this point, you may want to mirror some of their actions to see if this is welcome. Don't become a mime, but by copying a few of their behaviors, it shows that you are willing to learn and honor their ways.

Allow them to observe you, as well. Let them look at you and ask telepathic questions about the various aspects of your life. You may smell really strange to them, as the food you eat may emanate out of your pores (especially garlic and onions), and your lotions, make up, soap and shampoo will give off a scent. If you use a lot of synthetic fragrances, such as chemically scented laundry soap and dryer sheets, this may be overwhelming and be really offensive to someone from another planet.

Remember that it is important to come from a place of service. Ask how you may be of service to them, and ensure that this is heartfelt. ET's are very adept at detecting false motives and lies, so be honest and open in your communications and intentions.

Finally, show gratitude for their visit. Thank them for making contact with you and invite them to contact you again. Appreciate any messages or knowledge that they were willing to share with you, and be grateful for traveling so far to connect with you.

Don't forget to journal your experiences as soon as possible!

Now that you have some background and tools for interaction, let's learn about some basic, universal protocols for meeting with aliens.

## CHAPTER RECAP

As a sovereign human being, you are recognizing that you are grounded in your earth experience, while enabling yourself to raise your vibration and energy fields to communicate with beings from higher dimensions.  Your goal should be to:

1.) Come from a loving space;

2.) Set the intention to be of service;

3.) Observe them and allow them to observe you;

4.) Listen to what they have to say to you;

5.) Share information or knowledge with them;

6.) Thank them, be grateful for contact and any knowledge that they shared with you; and,

7.) Document your experiences.

# CHAPTER THIRTEEN

# Contact!  What To Do When You Connect

The moment is finally here!  You are meeting a non-human from another planet for the first time.  You are excited, scared and you freeze.  Then, you remember that you have been practicing your alien ETiquette™, exactly as you would prepare for an emergency!

ETiquette follows the same rules that Austrian attorney and father of space law, Ernst Fasan, speaks of regarding "Metalaw."  Metalaw states there is a prohibition against harming races living in outer space and that they, too, have the right to life and liberty.  Basically, treat others as you'd like to be treated.

On earth, a polite gesture or phrase in one culture may be considered rude in another culture, regardless of the good intentions of the person making the greeting.  Therefore, to successfully navigate cross-cultural first-time meetings, you need to study the customs.  Unfortunately, with regards to first-time ET encounters, there are no guidebooks available for studying how to make good first impressions, especially with countless different species in space.

After extensive research and interviews with sources whom have had encounters with various species, we are able to share a universal protocol that may be used in any contact experience:
- Be still, arms hanging by one's side with calm energy, mitigating any fear or over-enthusiasm one may have.  Breathe deeply, focus on your heart center and send LOVE to the being.

- Slowly raise either your right or left hand to shoulder height, palm facing out, as if you were taking an oath.   Some ET species will greet you by raising their right hand (e.g., the Pleadians taught this to the Native Americans) and the Apunians will greet you by raising their left hand.  The raising of your hand allows others to read your light signature and also indicate that you have no weapons in your hand.
- Observe the ET with soft focus (staring intensely can evoke defensive reactions) and relaxed facial features.  You may be startled by their physical appearance or surprised by the unexpected meeting.
- Unlike human interactions, the ET will most likely communicate with you telepathically.  If you have not yet experienced this communication style, you will begin to hear words in your head that are not your own thoughts, see pictures of things, or receive full-blown conversations.  You simply reply back in the same manner, by sending your thoughts and messages to them silently.
- With discerning judgment, follow their lead by gently and slowly imitating their actions or gestures.

The protocol above (perhaps even including telepathy) is also extremely successful when dealing with humans in cross-cultural encounters where neither party can communicate by common language.  Try practicing this protocol on your fellow humans in anticipation of your first ET encounter.

# CHAPTER FOURTEEN

# Journal Your Contacts & Dreams

Chapter Six discussed the importance of journaling your dreams, but I want to reiterate that contact during sleep is one of the first ways that you may be met by our galactic neighbors.

This is a safe space in which they can let you look at them and feel their energy so that you are not as afraid when you meet them in person. They are also able to impart messages, show that they are non-threatening, communicate with you telepathically, and perhaps show off their spacecrafts or technology.

You may also receive contact from our ET friends during meditation, or they may play music that reminds you of them. I have a friend who hears the opening five notes of the Close Encounters theme when she is receiving ET contact, and others have heard it while they are with her!

I will receive messages that are "downloads," or a sudden rush of information and inspiration. The entire concept for Galactic Ambassadors was dropped into my head on April 1, 2017 while Bill was out on a camping expedition. I then spent the rest of the day writing down the information that was flowing out of my head and drawing diagrams to support the overall project. By the time Bill got home, I had a blueprint for our project, and we then put a plan together to make it come to life.

No matter how you are receiving contact from our non-human neighbors, always remember to document your contact in a journal, including the day of the week, the date and time. Jot down the experience in as much detail as you can remember, and draw pictures and diagrams, if you can. You may also keep your journal on the computer if that is easier for you, but I seem to enjoy putting a pen to paper and savoring the process of scribing my encounters.

It is always fascinating to go back and re-read my journals to see where messages have been validated, or their inspiration or guidance that has manifested in my life. I feel that contact is a gift and should be treated as such, so logging my experiences and messages is a way to honor every encounter.

CHAPTER FIFTEEN

# Get Out There
# And Make Contact

Today, more than ever, it is easy to join like-minded individuals in making contact. Below are some suggested groups and resources that will support your efforts to connect with our benevolent galactic friends.

## Sky Watches and CE-5 Groups
There are CE-5 groups all over the world who use Dr. Stephen Greer's contact protocols on a monthly basis to send loving intentions to ET's in an attempt to connect (www.siriusdisclosure.com ). There are also ET Lets Talk groups that do sky watches on a regular basis, as well (www.etletstalk.com). Look for a local group that is going out to do a contact protocol and join them for an evening under the stars. Or, simply sit in your own backyard and make the intention to connect.

## UFO Organizations
An international organization called the Mutual UFO Network (MUFON) (www.mufon.com) provides over 50 years worth of research into the UFO phenomenon on their database, which is free to the public. They also have information about local MUFON chapters (e.g., www.mufonoc.org ) who hold monthly meetings in your neighborhood, and can help you to become a certified MUFON Field Investigator. You can hear amazing speakers who share the latest UFO research or sighting reports, and meet others who have had UFO or contact experience.

## UFO Conferences

There are conferences all over the world that celebrate the UFO phenomenon and ET contact. In the US alone, there are at least two or three major events happening each month, and there seems to be more new conferences each year. Some of our favorites include:

- Starworks USA, held in Laughlin, Nevada each year in early November. This intimate, three-day conference focuses on consciousness and its relation to UFOs and our galactic neighbors. They have top-notch international speakers presenting the latest research, amazing stories of contact, and a chance to interact with the presenters. (www.starworksusa.com )
- MUFON Symposium, held once a year in July in various locations rotating between the east coast, west coast, and Las Vegas. They also feature leading figures in UFO-logy and expert panels on trending topics. (www.mufon.com)
- Ricardo Gonzales Retreat, held annually in Crestone, Colorado in August. This gathering is limited to 100 participants and sells out within days. Attendees are immersed in the experiences of Ricardo Gonzales of Peru, who has had direct contact with the Apunian's, who are a race of 10 foot tall beings from the planet Apu. He has traveled the world on behalf of these emissaries from space, and shares his adventures regarding his mission for world peace. The conference features meditations, sky watches and messages from Antarel, his Apunian contact. Registration usually opens in early April for this conference in August. (www.starworksusa.com )
- AlienCon is held in various locations throughout the US, but we attend the gathering in Los Angeles, California. The event in LA occurs in

June, but check out the AlienCon website for a venue that is near to you. This event features the nuts and bolts data of UFO's and contact, while also providing the Hollywood glitz and glam of TV shows with UFO themes, and the latest historic intel on Ancient Alients from the History Channel. You will find a lot of people dressed up as Aliens, celebrating contact of all varieties. It's a great conference that balances real-world UFO experiences with light-hearted alien-lover fun. In addition, it is refreshing to see a wide representation of human races, ages and creeds coming together to celebrate our ET friends while overcoming all earthly divisions. (www.thealiencon.com)

**UFO Reference Materials**
With the internet, it has never been easier to research anything you want to know about UFO's, aliens, people who have had experiences with ET's, etc. However, you will want to use your personal discernment to evaluate people's claims and experiences. Keep an open mind, but ensure that you validate and verify information whenever possible. There are some "hoaxers" out there!

Books regarding the UFO phenomenon are sometimes available at your local library. However, Amazon.com and the MUFON.com websites have extensive books and DVD's for purchase that run the entire gamut, from historical UFO cases to government cover-up stories, to how to build a space ship!

The good news is you are not alone in your quest to learn more about our galactic neighbors and their crafts! Make the effort to connect with other curious humans as we all learn more about our non-human friends.

# CHAPTER SIXTEEN

# The Future Is In Your Hands

In order for us to become galactic citizens, we must come from a place of love and peace. The universe demands it. We must start with ourselves.

**BRING YOUR CURIOSITY** and explore the customs and cultures of our space neighbors.

**RAISE YOUR CONSCIOUSNESS** by taking personal responsibility for your:
- Diet
- Exercise
- Sleep
- Meditation
- Detoxification & Healing
- Truthfulness & Transparency
- Home Environment

Know that when you upgrade one area of your life, the other areas will demand that you "level up," as well. It is continual self-improvement as you move through life. This effect vibrates out through your family, your work, your community, the world, the universe, and the multi-verse. Be the pebble that makes a positive ripple of goodness through the waves of time and space.

**MAKE CONTACT** with your fellow humans and non-humans! Join an international cultural group for humans, or seek out a CE-5 group to reach out to the universe. Feel confident that you may approach ANY being with love, compassion, curiosity, joy and a sense of wonder.

The steps below are useful when making contact with non-humans:
As a sovereign human being, you are recognizing that you are grounded in your earth experience, while enabling yourself to raise your vibration and energy fields to communicate with beings from higher dimensions. Your goal should be to:
    1.) Come from a loving space;
    2.) Set the intention to be of service;
    3.) Observe them and allow them to observe you;
    4.) Listen to what they have to say to you;
    5.) Share information or knowledge with them;
    6.) Thank them, be grateful for contact and any knowledge that they shared with you; and,
    7.) Document your experiences.

I hope that this guide has provided you with inspiration, tools and protocols to enable contact with benevolent galactic beings. I am looking forward to hearing about your adventures at www.galacticambassadors.com.

# Guided Meditation With The Intention To Connect To Benevolent Galactic Beings

I would like to invite you to log onto the Galactic Ambassadors website (www.galacticambassadors.com ) to download the MP3 of a free guided meditation that I wrote and recorded.

Relax to the tranquil harp music and set the intention to connect with benevolent Galactic Beings.

If you prefer, you may review a transcript of the meditation below and set your own intention to connect.

**TRANSCRIPT OF GUIDED MEDITATION:**

Welcome to the Galactic Ambassadors Guided Meditation. Our intention is to connect with benevolent galactic beings, and share consciousness while being of service.

Please sit somewhere comfortable with your feet flat on the floor, your spine straight, and you hands are resting comfortably on your thighs.

Close your eyes.

Take a deep breath, hold it for the count of three and slowly exhale.

Again, take a deep breath, hold it for the count of three, and slowly exhale.

Envision that you have a cord coming out of your heart center. Send that cord down into the center of Gaia and wrap it around a huge quartz crystal.

Now envision that you have two cords coming out of your feet, and send those cords down into the center of Gaia and wrap them around two more large quarts crystals.

From those cords, bring up beautiful grounded earth energy up through your feet, up your legs, up through your spine, and out the top of your head. Breathe in through your nose and out through your mouth. "Gaia, we connect our crystalline core with your 5D through 12D crystalline core, as one, as one as one." Now, pull the energy up from Gaia's core, up through your body, up to your higher self, the sun, the central sun, and up to Divine Source. Take a deep breath in, and let it out.

From Divine Source, I want you to bring down beautiful crystalline white gold energy, bring it right down through the top of your head, down your spine, your legs, and send it right into the earth. Take a nice deep breath and exhale.

Envision that you have a gorgeous bubble of pure, crystalline light around you. "We close off our aura to all but our higher selves, and those beings of the highest vibration that are with us at the choice of our soul." So be it, and so it is. Take a nice deep breath in, and let it out.

Focus your attention on your heart center and take another deep breath. "Heart center, open and expand out to your light body." Exhale.

Take another deep breath, and expand your consciousness out to the universe level. Exhale.

Now breath in again, and expand your energy out to the multi-verse....feeling your entire being opening wider and wider. Exhale.

Take another deep breath, and merge with the Galactic levels. Feel the calm, peaceful space. Exhale, and take another breath.

While you are in this beautiful, safe and peaceful space, set the intention to connect to Galactic family and friends. SAY the following INVOCATION out loud: "I am now connecting........ with benevolent Galactic beings....... who wish to communicate with me.......... and my higher self........., in mutual service........., for the highest good of all. ....... So be it, and so it is."

Take a nice deep breath in, and exhale. Open yourself to contact in this present moment, or at a future time. (WAIT 2-3 minutes)

Bring your focus back to yourself, take a breath in through your nose, and blow it out of your mouth. Bring your awareness back to the Multi-Verse level.......... the Universe level...............and back down to earth. Take another deep breath, and blow out of your mouth in 7 quick puffs. You are now fully back in your body. Wiggle your hands and feet. Gently move your head and neck. When you are ready, open your eyes.

Welcome home. Please remember to journal your experience today. We hope you enjoyed this guided meditation.

**MEDITATION NOTE**: You may see someone, hear something, or feel emotions or feelings. When you make contact, welcome them. Ask them their name, or where they are from. Do they have a message for you? Ask them if you may be of service to them. When you are finished, thank your visitor for connecting with you, knowing that you are always able to connect with them again in the future.

# RESOURCES

Be sure to visit the Galactic Ambassadors website at www.galacticambassadors.com. The site includes additional resources, free guided meditation downloads and other awesome tidbits to help your journey.

Our mission is to:

- Share knowledge, wisdom, tools and resources that may assist to raise consciousness.

- Partner with others to share personal experiences, protocols and ETtiquette when meeting and greeting our galactic neighbors (and our fellow humans!)

- Sponsor or participate in events that raise consciousness, support research in the UFO phenomenon, or enable contact with our space brothers and sisters.

## SPIRITUAL GROWTH / CONSCIOUSNESS / THE SOUL'S JOURNEY

| Author | Title |
|---|---|
| David R. Hawkins | • Letting Go: The Pathway of Surrender<br>• Transcending the Levels of Consciousness |
| Don Miguel Ruiz | The Four Agreements |
| Jim Self and Roxanne Burnett | Spirit Matters |
| Lynne McTaggart | • The Intention Experiment<br>• The Field<br>• The Power of 8 |

| James Redfield | The Celestine Vision (and all books in the series) |
|---|---|
| Jacqueline Freeman | The Song of Increase |
| Marianne Williamson | A Course in Miracles |
| Michael Newton | • Destiny of Souls<br>• Journey of Souls<br>• Life Between Lives<br>(any books by him) |
| Brian Weiss, MD | Messages from the Masters (any books by him) |
| Caroline Myss | Sacred Contracts |
| Dan Millman | The Life You Were Born To Live |

## PSYCHIC AND EMPATH DEVELOPMENT

| Author | Title |
|---|---|
| Judith Orloff, MD | Second Sight |
| Rose Rosetree | Empowered by Empathy |
| Sonia Choquette, Ph. D | The Psychic Pathway |
| Sylvia Browne | Life on the Other Side / The Other Side and Back |
| James Van Prague | Heaven and Earth (any books by him) |
| John Edward | One Last Time (any books/tapes by him) |

## NUTRITION / DIET / HEALTH

| Author | Title |
|---|---|
| Ann Boroch, CNC | • The Candida Cure<br>• The Candida Cure Cookbook |
| Susan Schenk | Beyond Broccoli |
| Dr. Patricia Fitzgerald | The Detox Solution |
| Dr. Theodore A. Baroody | Alkalize or Die |
| Dr. Bernard Jensen | Dr. Jensen's Guide to Better Bowel Care |

## ALTERNATIVE HEALTH MODALITIES

| Type | Resources |
|---|---|
| Colonics | www.i-act.org (locate an IACT certified colon hydrotherapist) |
| Directional Non Force Technique Chiropractic | www.dnftchiropractic.com (locate a DNFT professional in your area) |

## THEOSOPHY AND MYSTERY SCHOOL TEACHINGS

| Author | Title |
|---|---|
| Alice A. Bailey | • Telepathy<br>• A Treatise on White Magic |
| Henry S. Olcott | Old Diary Leaves |
| Mark and Claire Prophet | Saint Germain on Alchemy |
| Godfre' Ray King | Unveiled Mysteries (and two others) |

## THE ASCENSION PROCESS

| Type | Resources |
|---|---|
| • Ascension Path Course ($)<br>• Light Intel Newsletter (free)<br>• Ascension materials (free)<br>• SUNday Unity Meditations (free) | www.SandraWalter.com Sandra Walter provides Ascension tools, resources and sessions to assist with the Ascension process. |

## MEDITATION

| Type | Resources |
| --- | --- |
| Transcendental Meditation ($) | www.TM.org |
| SUNday Unity Meditations (free) | www.SandraWalter.com |
| Guided Meditation to connect with benevolent galactic beings, guides and angels (free) | www.Galacticambassadors.com |

## UFO's, EXTRATERRESTRIALS, BIGFOOT, ETC.

| Author | Title |
| --- | --- |
| Paula Leopizzi Harris | Connecting the Dots |
| Richard Dolan | UFO's for the 21st Century Mind |
| Ingo Swann | Penetration: The Question of Extraterrestrial and Human Telepathy |
| Miguel Mendonca and Barbara Lamb | Meet The Hybrids: The Lives and Missions of E.T. Ambassadors on Earth |
| Colin Andrews | On The Edge of Reality |
| Stuart Holroyd | Briefing For The Landing On Planet Earth |
| Clifford Stone | Eyes Only – UFO Crash Retrievals |
| Ricardo Gonzales | Contact from Planet Apu: Beings from the future among us |
| Michel Zirger | We are here! Visitors Without a Passport |
| David Paulides | The Hoopa Project (Bigfoot sightings) Tribal Bigfoot |
| Preston Dennett | Not From Here |
| Robert W. Morgan | Bigfoot Observer's Field Manual |

| Joe Beelart and Cliff Olson | The Oregon Bigfoot Highway |
|---|---|
| J. La Tulippe, B.A | The UFO/Bigfoot Connection (Chapter 18, only) |
| William F. Hamilton, III | Project Aquarius |
| Orfeo M. Angelucci | The Secret of the Saucers |
| Truman Bethurum | Aboard a Flying Saucer |
| Jones and Smith | Voices From The Cosmos |
| William J. Birnes and Philip Corso | The Day After Roswell |
| Rey Hernandez | Beyond UFO's |

## UFO RELATED ORGANIZATIONS & CONFERENCES

| Type: | Resources: |
|---|---|
| **Mutual UFO Network (MUFON)** International organization that researches, investigates and provides education about the UFO Phenomenon. Report a UFO sighting, become a member, & Field Investigator training. | www.MUFON.com |
| **MUFON Symposium** Annual MUFON conference on UFO-logy that features the most current speakers and hot topics of the moment. | www.MUFON.com |

| | |
|---|---|
| **MUFON Orange County**, our local Costa Mesa, CA chapter of MUFON International, features some of the top names in UFO-logy speaking at monthly meetings. Held every third Wednesday of the month at the Costa Mesa Senior Center. Doors open at 7:00 p.m.<br>$10 for first time attendees, MUFON OC members/students, $15 for non-members.<br>Come see us at the registration desk and say hello! | www.MUFONOC.org |
| **STARWORKS USA**<br>A fantastic conference held in early November in Laughlin, Nevada that focuses on consciousness as an important factor in the UFO/ET phenomenon. Top UFO-logy speakers from around the world in an intimate setting where you can meet and talk with them after their presentations. Affordable conference fee and beautiful hotel rooms at ridiculously cheap prices. This is one conference that you MUST go to!<br>Executive Produced by Paola Harris, the renowned ET journalist and author. | www.starworksusa.com |

| Alien Con | www.thealiencon.com |
|---|---|
| What more can we say? This conference is all about making fans of ET's happy, and this event is awesome! A mix of beloved television-related UFO shows and the "real deal." Opportunities to attend various panels and presentations, have a photo op or get an autograph, and shop for the alien lover on your holiday list! | |

# ABOUT THE AUTHOR

**Tamara Scott Crowley** has enjoyed exploring and participating in the paranormal since childhood. At the age of five, she witnessed three UFO's (saucer type) chasing each other in a triangular shape in the skies over Portland, Oregon in the middle of the night with her grandfather, grandmother and little sister. Over the years, she has had many UFO sightings – including an incredible display on her birthday in Mt. Shasta, CA with her husband and a wonderful friend. She will also share her personal Sasquatch sighting if you ask her about it. To her, the "paranormal" is normal, and every new experience is one of awe and wonderment!

Tamara is an empath, as well as a Spiritual Medium, and her skills have enabled her to serve as a conduit between time/space/dimensions/people. She has used her gifts to assist law enforcement with searches for missing people, and has conducted more than 500 readings for private clients. Tamara feels that being a medium is a sacred gift, and it is important to come from your heart, and be a "clear channel" in service to others. The web site for this work may be found at: www.tamarascottcrowley.com

She is the visionary and co-founder (with her husband, Bill Crowley) of Galactic Ambassadors, whose mission is to prepare earth's citizens for contact with our galactic neighbors! Visit their website at www.galacticambassadors.com to:
- Enjoy a FREE guided meditation to connect with non-human species;
- Access knowledge, wisdom, tools and resources that may assist to raise consciousness;

- Learn protocols and ETtiquette when meeting and greeting our galactic neighbors (and our fellow humans!); and,
- Discover events that raise consciousness, support research in the UFO phenomenon, or enable contact with our space brothers and sisters.

Tamara is a graduate of Oregon State University in Corvallis, Oregon, and holds a Bachelor of Science degree in Technical Journalism. She had a successful career in Corporate Communications for various Fortune 200 companies, such as Countrywide Financial Corporation and Toyota Financial Services, in addition to public service for various local governments in Oregon and Washington State. She co-founded a commuter airline, and has also worked extensively in the Investment Real Estate industry.

In her spare time, she plays the Celtic harp, and volunteers as a MUFON Field Investigator and MUFON Orange County Board Member.

# ACKNOWLEDGEMENTS

There have been so many wonderful individuals who have helped me on my path, as well as with this book.

My husband, Bill Crowley, and best friend, Don Rich, have been my champions ever since the concept for Galactic Ambassadors was "downloaded" to me on April 1, 2017. "Prepare For Contact" was an integral piece of the project, and their feedback and guidance during the concept, review and editing phase made the book what it is today. Their ongoing support, creativity and collaboration are reflected in every aspect of Galactic Ambassadors, and I am so thankful for their ongoing partnership.

There are so many within the UFO community who have generously given their time and energy to this book and the Galactic Ambassadors mission: Paola Harris, Dr. Bob Wood and Barbara Lamb for their contributions and lovely support of "Prepare For Contact;" the MUFON Orange County Board; the MUFON International organization and Executive Director, Jan Harzan; my fellow MUFON Field Investigators; and Richard and Tracey Dolan who encouraged our vision while we were in Uluru. Thanks to all of you for your support, guidance and shared love of positive non-human contact.

There have been many gifted healers who have helped me on my journey, and I am grateful for their knowledge, intuition and patience while they guided me towards optimum health: James Allred and Madeline Angelus for their brilliance regarding colon hydrotherapy and energy medicine; Dr. Christopher John for his ongoing genius with DNFT Chiropractic methods; naturopath and acupuncturist Dr. Patricia Fitzgerald; and Dr. Leah Matson who was there for me during one of the biggest transitions of my life. You have all played an integral role in my ongoing evolution and have shaped my trajectory. Thanks to all of you!

My first UFO encounter was at the age of five with my late grandparents, Ralph and Frankie Greener, and my sister, Michelle. Thank you for sharing my initiation into UFOlogy, the paranormal, and the mysteries of life and beyond.

Many thanks to my family, and to Carmen Aguilar @carmenaguilarphoto for the beautiful headshot for the book. Finally, I am especially grateful to my cat, Sparky, who spent many hours snoozing on my lap while I was writing this book.

Made in the USA
Middletown, DE
03 March 2023